LAZY COOKBOOK
RECIPES

Copyright

© Copyright 2025 - Samantha Reed All rights reserved.
No part of this book may be reproduced, distributed, or transmitted in any form or by any means, including photocopying, recording, or other electronic or mechanical methods, without the prior written permission of the publisher, except in the case of brief quotations used in book reviews and certain other noncommercial uses permitted by copyright law.

LAZY COOKBOOK RECIPES

100 QUICK & DELICIOUS RECIPES FOR BUSY PEOPLE, BEGINNERS, AND LAZY COOKS - MINIMAL INGREDIENTS, MAXIMUM FLAVOR!

SAMANTHA REED

INTRODUCTION

We've all been there—long days, endless to-do lists, and the constant struggle to figure out what's for dinner. Cooking can feel overwhelming when you're short on time, energy, and patience. That's exactly why *Lazy Cookbook Recipes: 100 Quick & Delicious Recipes for Busy People, Beginners, and Lazy Cooks – Minimal Ingredients, Maximum Flavor!* was created. This book is designed for those who love good food but don't want to spend hours in the kitchen. Whether you're a busy professional, a parent juggling multiple responsibilities, or simply someone who prefers efficiency over elaborate meal prep, this cookbook will become your go-to guide for quick, delicious, and stress-free meals.

Why This Cookbook?

In today's fast-paced world, convenience is key. But convenience doesn't have to mean unhealthy takeout or bland frozen meals. This cookbook is all about balancing speed, simplicity, and nutrition. Every recipe in this book is:

- **Quick**: Ready in 15 to 30 minutes.
- **Easy**: No complicated techniques or hard-to-find ingredients.
- **Minimalist**: Uses a handful of pantry staples to create satisfying meals.

With these recipes, you'll be able to whip up flavorful breakfasts, lunches, and dinners without spending unnecessary time chopping, measuring, or waiting for food to cook.

Time-Saving Hacks for Effortless Cooking

To truly embrace the "lazy cook" lifestyle, efficiency is everything. Here are a few tried-and-true strategies to make meal prep even faster:

> **Meal Prep Smartly:** Spend 30 minutes on the weekend washing, chopping, and portioning ingredients. Store prepped veggies in airtight containers, marinate proteins in advance, and pre-cook grains for quick assembly.
> **One-Pan & One-Pot Wonders**: Cut down on cleanup by choosing recipes that require minimal cookware. Sheet pan meals, skillet dishes, and instant pot recipes save both time and effort.
> **Batch Cooking**: Double up on certain recipes like soups, stews, or sauces and freeze leftovers in portioned containers for future easy meals.
> **Use Pre-Cut or Frozen Ingredients**: Pre-cut vegetables, frozen fruits, and canned beans can significantly reduce prep time while still offering great nutrition.
> **Keep a Well-Stocked Pantry**: Having versatile staples like olive oil, spices, canned tomatoes, rice, and pasta on hand means you can throw together a meal without making a last-minute grocery run.

Storage Tips for Maximum Freshness
The secret to making quick meals even easier is having ingredients ready to go. Here's how to store them efficiently:
- **Vegetables & Herbs:** Store fresh herbs in a glass of water in the fridge or freeze them in olive oil using an ice cube tray for easy seasoning.
- **Protein:** Keep portions of chicken, fish, or tofu frozen in individual bags for easy thawing.
- **Grains & Pasta:** Cook in bulk and store in the fridge for up to 4 days, or freeze portions for quick reheating.
- **Cheese & Dairy:** Grate cheese ahead of time and store in an airtight container for faster use.

How to Make the Most of This Cookbook
This cookbook is divided into two main sections: **15-Minute Meals** and **30-Minute Meals**—because we know that some days you need a lightning-fast fix, while other days you can spare a few extra minutes. Each section includes recipes for breakfast, lunch, and dinner, making it easy to mix and match meals that fit your schedule.

Each recipe includes:
- **Clear, step-by-step instructions** – No over-complicated techniques.
- **Minimal ingredients** – Only what's necessary to make the meal delicious.
- **Nutrition information** – To help you stay mindful of your intake.

Cooking should never feel like a chore. With the right approach, it can be simple, enjoyable, and most importantly, quick. So grab your ingredients, turn on some music, and let's make cooking effortless! Happy cooking!

Samantha Reed

INGREDIENTS AND POSSIBLE SUBSTITUTES FROM LAZY COOKBOOK RECIPES

Grains & Bread
- **Whole wheat tortilla:** Substitute: Regular flour tortilla, corn tortilla, lettuce wrap
- **Whole grain bread:** Substitute: Rye bread, sourdough, gluten-free bread
- **English muffin:** Substitute: Whole wheat bun, bagel, gluten-free muffin
- **Rice cakes: Substitute:** Whole grain crackers, oatcakes
- **Ziti pasta: Substitute:** Penne, rigatoni, fusilli
- **Quinoa:** Substitute: Brown rice, bulgur, couscous
- **Brown rice:** Substitute: White rice, farro, barley
- **Oats (rolled oats):** Substitute: Instant oats, steel-cut oats, quinoa flakes

Dairy & Dairy Alternatives
- **Milk (dairy or non-dairy):** Substitute: Almond milk, soy milk, oat milk, coconut milk
- **Greek yogurt:** Substitute: Regular yogurt, skyr, coconut yogurt
- **Cottage cheese:** Substitute: Ricotta cheese, feta cheese, soft tofu
- **Cheddar cheese:** Substitute: Colby cheese, gouda, mozzarella
- **Mozzarella cheese:** Substitute: Provolone, burrata, feta
- **Parmesan cheese:** Substitute: Pecorino Romano, nutritional yeast
- **Cream cheese:** Substitute: Mascarpone, ricotta, cashew cream

Protein Sources
- **Eggs:** Substitute: Silken tofu (for scrambled eggs), flaxseed or chia egg (for baking)
- **Chicken breast:** Substitute: Turkey breast, tofu, tempeh
- **Ground turkey:** Substitute: Ground chicken, lean ground beef, lentils
- **Salmon (fresh or canned):** Substitute: Tuna, trout, mackerel
- **Tilapia:** Substitute: Cod, haddock, halibut
- **Shrimp:** Substitute: Scallops, tofu, chickpeas
- **Canned tuna:** Substitute: Canned salmon, shredded chicken, mashed chickpeas
- **Canned chickpeas:** Substitute: Black beans, white beans, lentils
- **Black beans:** Substitute: Kidney beans, pinto beans, chickpeas
- **Ground beef:** Substitute: Ground turkey, plant-based meat, mushrooms
- **Tofu (firm or silken):** Substitute: Tempeh, paneer, seitan

Vegetables
- **Avocado:** Substitute: Mashed peas, hummus, cashew cream
- **Spinach:** Substitute: Kale, Swiss chard, arugula
- **Zucchini:** Substitute: Cucumber (raw), eggplant (cooked)
- **Bell pepper:** Substitute: Poblano pepper, carrots, celery
- **Cherry tomatoes:** Substitute: Grape tomatoes, regular diced tomatoes
- **Cucumber:** Substitute: Zucchini (raw), celery
- **Sweet potatoes:** Substitute: Pumpkin, butternut squash, regular potatoes
- **Onions (red or white):** Substitute: Shallots, leeks, green onions

INGREDIENTS AND POSSIBLE SUBSTITUTES FROM LAZY COOKBOOK RECIPES

Fruits
- **Banana:** Substitute: Applesauce, mashed avocado
- **Berries (strawberries, blueberries, raspberries, etc.):** Substitute: Chopped peaches, cherries, dried fruit (soaked)
- **Pineapple:** Substitute: Mango, papaya, canned peaches
- **Apple:** Substitute: Pear, nectarine, banana

Condiments & Seasonings
- **Olive oil:** Substitute: Avocado oil, coconut oil, canola oil
- **Soy sauce:** Substitute: Tamari, coconut aminos, Worcestershire sauce
- **Balsamic vinegar:** Substitute: Apple cider vinegar, red wine vinegar
- **Lemon juice:** Substitute: Lime juice, white vinegar
- **Garlic powder:** Substitute: Fresh minced garlic, onion powder
- **Paprika:** Substitute: Smoked paprika, cayenne pepper
- **Chili powder:** Substitute: Cumin + cayenne pepper mix
- **Hummus:** Substitute: Baba ganoush, mashed avocado, Greek yogurt dip
- **Pesto:** Substitute: Chimichurri, tahini sauce, herbed olive oil
- **Peanut butter:** Substitute: Almond butter, sunflower seed butter, cashew butter
- **Honey:** Substitute: Maple syrup, agave syrup, date syrup
- **Mustard (Dijon or yellow):** Substitute: Horseradish, wasabi, honey mustard

This list provides easy ingredient swaps for various recipes from the Lazy Cookbook, ensuring flexibility and accessibility based on dietary preferences or pantry availability.

TABLE OF CONTENTS

Introduction	4
Ingredients and Possible Substitutes from Lazy Cookbook Recipes	6

15-MINUTE MEALS — 11

Berry Blast Instant Oats	12
Peanut Butter Banana Wrap	13
3-Ingredient Avocado Toast	14
Strawberry Almond Smoothie	15
Cottage Cheese & Honey Toast	16
Instant Chia Pudding	17
Apple & Almond Butter Rice Cakes	18
Banana Yogurt Parfait	19
5-Minute Scrambled Eggs with Cheese	20
5-Minute Avocado & Egg Toast	21
Quick Chocolate Protein Shake	22
Microwave Mug Omelet	23
Berry Yogurt Smoothie	24
Quick Cottage Cheese & Fruit Bowl	25
Instant 3-Ingredient Chia Pudding	26
Apple & Almond Butter Toast	27
Microwave Oatmeal with Nuts & Honey	28
Quick Nutty Banana Oats	29
Quick Breakfast Burrito	30
Classic Turkey & Cheese Sandwich	31
Avocado Tuna Salad Wrap	32
Chickpea & Cucumber Salad	33
Quick Caprese Salad	34
Greek Yogurt Chicken Salad	35
Hummus & Veggie Wrap	36
Canned Salmon & Avocado Toast	37
Simple Egg Salad Sandwich	38
Spicy Black Bean & Cheese Quesadilla	39
Quick Pita Pocket with Chicken & Veggies	40
Quick & Easy Cucumber Yogurt Salad	41
Chicken & Rice Bowl	42
Smoked Salmon & Cream Cheese Bagel	43
Egg & Avocado English Muffin	44
Caprese Avocado Toast	45
Cottage Cheese & Pineapple Bowl	46
Quick Asian-Inspired Chicken Wrap	47
Quick Italian Tuna Salad	48
Garlic Butter Shrimp & Zoodles	49
Cheesy Turkey & Spinach Skillet	50
One-Pan Lemon Garlic Chicken & Broccoli	51

TABLE OF CONTENTS

Turkey and Avocado Lettuce Wraps	52
Veggie and Hummus Wrap	53
Tomato Basil Mozzarella Skewers	54
Avocado & Tomato Toast	55
Greek Yogurt Parfait	56
Scrambled Eggs with Veggies	57
Mediterranean Hummus & Veggie Wrap	58
Quick Vegetable Stir-Fry	59
Simple Tuna Salad	60
Avocado & Black Bean Salad	61
Quinoa Veggie Stir-Fry	62
Garlic & Herb Shrimp Skillet	63

30-MINUTE MEALS — 64

Spinach & Feta Omelet	65
Banana Pancakes	66
Breakfast Skillet with Sausage & Potatoes	67
Quinoa & Chickpea Salad Bowl	68
Sweet Potato & Black Bean Chili	69
Lentil Soup with Spinach	70
Baked Lemon Herb Chicken	71
Salmon with Roasted Vegetables	72
Pesto Chicken Salad	73
Lemon Herb Roasted Chicken Breasts	74
One-Pan Baked Salmon with Veggies	75
Sweet Potato & Black Bean Tacos	76
Quick Beef Stir-Fry	77
Lemon Garlic Shrimp Pasta	78
Spicy Chicken & Veggie Skillet	79
Easy Baked Ziti	80
Chicken Caesar Wraps	81
Quick Veggie Stir-Fry with Tofu	82
Chicken and Spinach Alfredo	83
Quick Baked Tilapia with Lemon and Garlic	84
Pesto Chicken with Zucchini Noodles	85
Garlic Parmesan Roasted Shrimp	86
Spicy Chickpea and Quinoa Bowl	87
Simple Beef and Veggie Stir-Fry	88
Mediterranean Chicken Skewers with Tzatziki	89
Spinach and Cheese Stuffed Portobello Mushrooms	90
Quick Egg Fried Rice	91
Baked Chicken Thighs with Sweet Potatoes	92
Lemon Garlic Shrimp and Asparagus	93

TABLE OF CONTENTS

SAUCES, DRESSINGS & SIMPLE SEASONINGS — 94

Simple Tomato Sauce	95
Creamy Avocado Dressing	96
Garlic Butter Sauce	97
Sweet and Spicy Stir-Fry Sauce	98
Classic Vinaigrette Dressing	99
Lemon Herb Dressing	100
Tangy Yogurt Dressing	101
Basic Pesto Sauce	102
Peanut Butter Dipping Sauce	103
Balsamic Glaze	104
Quick Tomato Sauce	105
Avocado Lime Dressing	106
Spicy Sriracha Mayo	107
Garlic Parmesan Sauce	108
Simple Honey Mustard Dressing	109
Tangy Tahini Dressing	110
Classic Italian Herb Seasoning	111
5-Minute Peanut Butter Dipping Sauce	112
Simple Lemon Garlic Dressing	113
Sweet Chili Sauce	114

15-MINUTE MEALS

BERRY BLAST INSTANT OATS

INGREDIENTS

- ½ cup quick-cooking oats
- ½ cup milk (or any plant-based milk)
- ½ cup mixed fresh or frozen berries (strawberries, blueberries, raspberries)
- 1 tablespoon honey or maple syrup
- 1 tablespoon chia seeds (optional)
- 1 tablespoon Greek yogurt (optional for creaminess)
- A pinch of salt

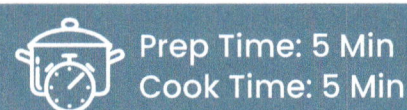 Prep Time: 5 Min
Cook Time: 5 Min

 Servings: 1

DIRECTIONS

1. In a microwave-safe bowl, add quick oats, milk, and a pinch of salt.
2. Microwave on high for 2–3 minutes.
3. Stir well, then add honey (or maple syrup), chia seeds, and Greek yogurt if using.
4. Add the mixed berries on top. If frozen, microwave for an extra 30 seconds.
5. Stir again and let sit for 1 minute to thicken.
6. Enjoy your lazy, delicious Berry Blast!

NUTRITION INFORMATION PER SERVING

Calories: 310 | Protein: 12g | Fat: 7g | Carbs: 48g

PEANUT BUTTER BANANA WRAP

INGREDIENTS
- 1 whole wheat tortilla
- 2 tbsp peanut butter
- 1 medium banana, sliced
- 1 tsp honey (optional)
- ½ tsp cinnamon

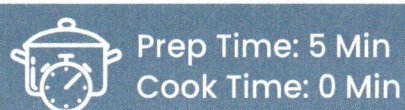 Prep Time: 5 Min
Cook Time: 0 Min

 Servings: 1

DIRECTIONS
1. Spread peanut butter evenly over the tortilla.
2. Arrange banana slices on top and drizzle with honey if desired.
3. Sprinkle with cinnamon, roll up the tortilla, and slice in half.
4. Enjoy immediately or wrap it for an on-the-go breakfast.

NUTRITION INFORMATION PER SERVING
Calories: 320 | Protein: 9g | Fat: 14g | Carbs: 42g

3-INGREDIENT AVOCADO TOAST

INGREDIENTS
- 1 slice whole grain bread
- ½ avocado, mashed
- 1 pinch sea salt

Prep Time: 5 Min
Cook Time: 0 Min

Servings: 1

DIRECTIONS
1. Toast the bread to your preferred crispiness.
2. Spread mashed avocado on top and sprinkle with sea salt.
3. Serve immediately and enjoy.

NUTRITION INFORMATION PER SERVING
Calories: 180 | Protein: 4g | Fat: 10g | Carbs: 20g

STRAWBERRY ALMOND SMOOTHIE

INGREDIENTS

- 1 cup almond milk (or any milk of choice)
- ½ cup frozen strawberries
- 1 tbsp almond butter
- 1 tsp honey or maple syrup (optional)
- ½ tsp vanilla extract
- ¼ cup Greek yogurt (optional for extra protein)

 Prep Time: 5 Min
Cook Time: 0 Min

 Servings: 1

DIRECTIONS

1. Add all ingredients into a blender. If using fresh strawberries, add a few ice cubes for a chilled texture.
2. Blend on high speed until smooth and creamy. If the smoothie is too thick, add a little more milk.
3. Taste and adjust sweetness if needed by adding honey or maple syrup.
4. Pour into a glass and enjoy immediately.

NUTRITION INFORMATION PER SERVING
Calories: 220 | Protein: 8g | Fat: 10g | Carbs: 26g

COTTAGE CHEESE & HONEY TOAST

INGREDIENTS
- 1 slice whole grain bread
- ½ cup cottage cheese
- 1 tsp honey
- 1 tbsp chopped nuts (almonds or walnuts)
- ¼ tsp cinnamon

Prep Time: 5 Min
Cook Time: 0 Min

Servings: 1

DIRECTIONS
1. Toast the bread until golden brown and crispy.
2. Spread the cottage cheese evenly on the warm toast.
3. Drizzle honey on top and sprinkle with chopped nuts and cinnamon.
4. Serve immediately and enjoy as a protein-packed breakfast.

NUTRITION INFORMATION PER SERVING
Calories: 200 | Protein: 12g | Fat: 5g | Carbs: 28g

INSTANT CHIA PUDDING

INGREDIENTS

- 3 tablespoons chia seeds
- ½ cup milk (any kind)
- 1 tablespoon honey or maple syrup
- ¼ teaspoon vanilla extract (optional)
- A handful of fresh berries or sliced banana
- A pinch of cinnamon (optional)

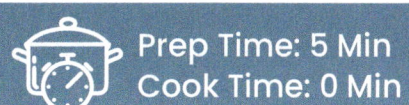 Prep Time: 5 Min
Cook Time: 0 Min

 Servings: 1

DIRECTIONS

1. In a bowl or jar, mix chia seeds, milk, honey (or maple syrup), and vanilla extract.
2. Stir well for about a minute, ensuring there are no clumps.
3. Let it sit on the counter for 5 minutes, stirring once halfway to help it thicken quickly.
4. Top with fresh berries or banana slices and a pinch of cinnamon if desired.
5. Dig in and enjoy your instant, no-wait chia pudding!

NUTRITION INFORMATION PER SERVING

Calories: 260 | Protein: 8g | Fat: 12g | Carbs: 28g

APPLE & ALMOND BUTTER RICE CAKES

INGREDIENTS
- 2 rice cakes
- 2 tbsp almond butter
- ½ apple, thinly sliced
- ½ tsp cinnamon
- 1 tsp honey (optional)

Prep Time: 5 Min
Cook Time: 0 Min

Servings: 1

DIRECTIONS
1. Spread almond butter evenly over each rice cake.
2. Arrange thin apple slices on top of the almond butter.
3. Sprinkle with cinnamon and drizzle with honey if desired.
4. Serve immediately as a crunchy, satisfying breakfast.

NUTRITION INFORMATION PER SERVING
Calories: 230 | Protein: 6g | Fat: 12g | Carbs: 28g

BANANA YOGURT PARFAIT

INGREDIENTS

- ½ cup Greek yogurt
- 1 small banana, sliced
- 2 tbsp granola
- 1 tsp honey
- 1 tbsp chopped nuts (almonds or walnuts)

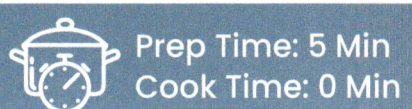 Prep Time: 5 Min
Cook Time: 0 Min

 Servings: 1

DIRECTIONS

1. In a glass or bowl, add half of the Greek yogurt as the first layer.
2. Add half of the banana slices on top of the yogurt.
3. Sprinkle 1 tablespoon of granola over the banana slices.
4. Repeat the layering with the remaining yogurt, banana slices, and granola.
5. Drizzle honey on top and garnish with chopped nuts for extra crunch.
6. Serve immediately and enjoy.

NUTRITION INFORMATION PER SERVING

Calories: 250 | Protein: 12g | Fat: 6g | Carbs: 38g

5-MINUTE SCRAMBLED EGGS WITH CHEESE

INGREDIENTS

- 2 large eggs
- 2 tbsp shredded cheese (cheddar, mozzarella, or your choice)
- 1 tbsp milk
- ½ tbsp butter or olive oil
- Salt and pepper to taste

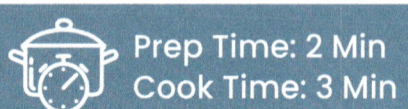
Prep Time: 2 Min
Cook Time: 3 Min

Servings: 1

DIRECTIONS

1. Crack the eggs into a bowl and whisk them with the milk, salt, and pepper.
2. Heat a non-stick pan over medium-low heat and add the butter or olive oil.
3. Pour the egg mixture into the pan and let it cook for about 30 seconds.
4. Using a spatula, gently stir and fold the eggs as they cook.
5. When the eggs are nearly set, sprinkle the shredded cheese over the top.
6. Stir until the cheese melts, then remove from heat and serve immediately.

NUTRITION INFORMATION PER SERVING

Calories: 220 | Protein: 14g | Fat: 16g | Carbs: 2g

5-MINUTE AVOCADO & EGG TOAST

INGREDIENTS

- 1 slice whole grain bread
- ½ avocado, mashed
- 1 egg
- ½ tbsp olive oil
- Salt and pepper to taste
- Red pepper flakes (optional)

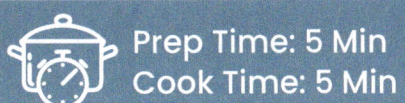 Prep Time: 5 Min
Cook Time: 5 Min

 Servings: 1

DIRECTIONS

1. Toast the bread until golden brown.
2. While the bread is toasting, heat a small pan over medium heat and add olive oil.
3. Crack the egg into the pan and cook until the whites are set but the yolk is slightly runny (or fully cooked if preferred).
4. Spread mashed avocado over the toasted bread and season with salt and pepper.
5. Place the cooked egg on top of the avocado.
6. Sprinkle with red pepper flakes if desired, and serve immediately.

NUTRITION INFORMATION PER SERVING

Calories: 280 | Protein: 10g | Fat: 18g | Carbs: 22g

QUICK CHOCOLATE PROTEIN SHAKE

INGREDIENTS

- 1 cup milk (dairy or non-dairy)
- 1 scoop chocolate protein powder
- 1 small banana
- 1 tbsp peanut butter
- ½ tsp cinnamon (optional)
- ½ cup ice cubes

Prep Time: 5 Min
Cook Time: 0 Min

Servings: 1

DIRECTIONS

1. Add all the ingredients to a blender.
2. Blend on high speed until smooth and creamy.
3. Taste and adjust sweetness if needed by adding a drizzle of honey.
4. Pour into a glass and enjoy immediately.

NUTRITION INFORMATION PER SERVING

Calories: 320 | Protein: 25g | Fat: 10g | Carbs: 40g

MICROWAVE MUG OMELET

INGREDIENTS

- 2 eggs
- 2 tbsp milk
- 2 tbsp shredded cheese
- ¼ cup diced vegetables (bell peppers, spinach, onions)
- Salt and pepper to taste

 Prep Time: 5 Min
Cook Time: 2 Min

 Servings: 1

DIRECTIONS

1. In a microwave-safe mug, whisk the eggs and milk together.
2. Stir in the shredded cheese and diced vegetables.
3. Season with salt and pepper.
4. Microwave on high for 1 minute, then stir the mixture.
5. Microwave for another 30 seconds to 1 minute, until the eggs are fully cooked.
6. Let it cool for a few seconds before eating.

NUTRITION INFORMATION PER SERVING

Calories: 210 | Protein: 16g | Fat: 12g | Carbs: 5g

BERRY YOGURT SMOOTHIE

INGREDIENTS
- 1 cup mixed berries (strawberries, blueberries, raspberries)
- ½ cup Greek yogurt
- ½ cup milk (or non-dairy alternative)
- 1 tbsp honey or maple syrup
- ½ tsp vanilla extract
- ½ cup ice cubes

 Prep Time: 5 Min
Cook Time: 0 Min

 Servings: 1

DIRECTIONS
1. Add all ingredients to a blender.
2. Blend on high speed for 30–60 seconds until smooth.
3. If the smoothie is too thick, add a splash of milk and blend again.
4. Pour into a glass and serve immediately.

NUTRITION INFORMATION PER SERVING
Calories: 200 | Protein: 10g | Fat: 4g | Carbs: 35g

QUICK COTTAGE CHEESE & FRUIT BOWL

INGREDIENTS

- ½ cup cottage cheese
- ½ cup diced fruit (pineapple, mango, or berries)
- 1 tbsp chopped nuts (almonds, walnuts, or pecans)
- ½ tsp honey or maple syrup

Prep Time: 5 Min
Cook Time: 0 Min

Servings: 1

DIRECTIONS

1. Spoon the cottage cheese into a serving bowl.
2. Top with diced fruit of your choice.
3. Sprinkle chopped nuts over the fruit for crunch.
4. Drizzle honey or maple syrup over everything.
5. Serve immediately and enjoy!

NUTRITION INFORMATION PER SERVING

Calories: 180 | Protein: 15g | Fat: 5g | Carbs: 20g

INSTANT 3-INGREDIENT CHIA PUDDING

INGREDIENTS
- 3 tablespoons ground chia seeds (use pre-ground chia for faster thickening)
- ½ cup cold milk (any kind)
- 1 tablespoon honey or maple syrup

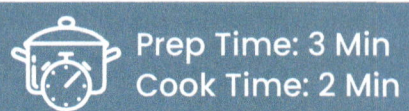
Prep Time: 3 Min
Cook Time: 2 Min

Servings: 1

DIRECTIONS
1. In a bowl or jar, combine ground chia seeds, cold milk, and honey (or maple syrup).
2. Stir well for about 1 minute until smooth and starting to thicken.
3. Let it sit for 2 minutes at room temperature, stirring once halfway.
4. The mixture will become pudding-like in texture — if too thick, add a splash of milk and stir again.
5. Eat immediately!

NUTRITION INFORMATION PER SERVING
Calories: 240 | Protein: 9g | Fat: 11g | Carbs: 23g

APPLE & ALMOND BUTTER TOAST

INGREDIENTS

- 1 slice whole grain bread
- 1 tbsp almond butter
- ½ apple, thinly sliced
- ¼ tsp cinnamon
- ½ tsp honey (optional)

Prep Time: 5 Min
Cook Time: 0 Min

Servings: 1

DIRECTIONS

1. Toast the whole grain bread until golden brown.
2. Spread almond butter evenly over the toast.
3. Arrange the apple slices on top of the almond butter.
4. Sprinkle with cinnamon and drizzle honey for added flavor.
5. Serve immediately.

NUTRITION INFORMATION PER SERVING

Calories: 220 | Protein: 6g | Fat: 10g | Carbs: 28g

MICROWAVE OATMEAL WITH NUTS & HONEY

INGREDIENTS

- ½ cup rolled oats
- 1 cup milk (or water)
- 1 tbsp chopped nuts (almonds, walnuts, or pecans)
- ½ tsp cinnamon
- 1 tsp honey

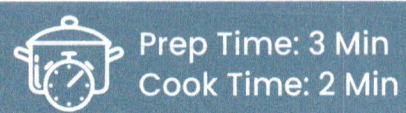
Prep Time: 3 Min
Cook Time: 2 Min

Servings: 1

DIRECTIONS

1. In a microwave-safe bowl, combine the rolled oats and milk.
2. Microwave on high for 1½ to 2 minutes, stirring halfway through.
3. Let the oatmeal sit for 1 minute to thicken.
4. Stir in cinnamon and top with chopped nuts.
5. Drizzle honey over the top and enjoy warm.

NUTRITION INFORMATION PER SERVING

Calories: 250 | Protein: 9g | Fat: 8g | Carbs: 35g

QUICK NUTTY BANANA OATS

INGREDIENTS

- ½ cup quick-cooking oats
- ½ cup milk (or any plant-based milk)
- 1 ripe banana, sliced
- 1 tablespoon peanut butter or almond butter
- 1 tablespoon chopped nuts (walnuts or almonds)
- ½ teaspoon cinnamon (optional)
- 1 teaspoon honey or maple syrup (optional)

 Prep Time: 5 Min
Cook Time: 3 Min

 Servings: 1

DIRECTIONS

1. In a microwave-safe bowl, combine quick oats and milk.
2. Microwave on high for 2–3 minutes.
3. Stir well, then add the sliced banana and peanut butter.
4. Sprinkle with cinnamon and chopped nuts.
5. Drizzle honey or maple syrup on top if desired.
6. Give it a final stir and enjoy warm — ready in minutes!

NUTRITION INFORMATION PER SERVING
Calories: 380 | Protein: 11g | Fat: 14g | Carbs: 48g

QUICK BREAKFAST BURRITO

INGREDIENTS
- 1 whole wheat tortilla
- 2 eggs, scrambled
- 2 tbsp shredded cheese
- 2 tbsp salsa
- ½ avocado, sliced

 Prep Time: 5 Min
Cook Time: 5 Min

 Servings: 1

DIRECTIONS
1. Scramble the eggs in a pan over medium heat until fully cooked.
2. Warm the tortilla in a dry pan or microwave for a few seconds.
3. Place the scrambled eggs in the center of the tortilla.
4. Sprinkle with shredded cheese and add sliced avocado.
5. Drizzle salsa over the filling, then roll up the tortilla tightly.
6. Serve immediately or wrap in foil for a quick on-the-go breakfast.

NUTRITION INFORMATION PER SERVING

Calories: 350 | Protein: 18g | Fat: 20g | Carbs: 30g

CLASSIC TURKEY & CHEESE SANDWICH

INGREDIENTS

- 2 slices whole wheat bread
- 3 oz sliced turkey breast
- 1 slice cheddar cheese
- 2 lettuce leaves
- 2 tomato slices
- 1 tbsp mustard or mayonnaise

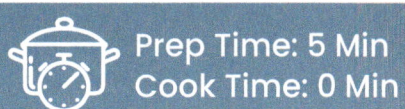
Prep Time: 5 Min
Cook Time: 0 Min

Servings: 1

DIRECTIONS

1. Spread mustard or mayonnaise on one side of each bread slice.
2. Layer turkey slices, cheese, lettuce, and tomato on one slice of bread.
3. Place the second slice of bread on top, press gently, and slice in half.
4. Serve immediately or wrap in foil for a quick grab-and-go lunch.

NUTRITION INFORMATION PER SERVING

Calories: 320 | Protein: 25g | Fat: 10g | Carbs: 35g

AVOCADO TUNA SALAD WRAP

INGREDIENTS
- 1 whole wheat tortilla
- 1 small avocado, mashed
- 1 can (5 oz) tuna, drained
- 1 tbsp Greek yogurt or mayonnaise
- ½ tsp lemon juice
- ¼ tsp salt and pepper
- 2 lettuce leaves

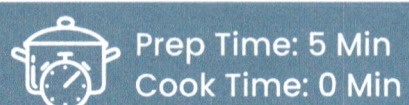
Prep Time: 5 Min
Cook Time: 0 Min

Servings: 1

DIRECTIONS
1. In a bowl, mix together the mashed avocado, tuna, Greek yogurt, lemon juice, salt, and pepper until well combined.
2. Spread the mixture evenly over the tortilla.
3. Place lettuce leaves on top and roll the tortilla tightly.
4. Slice in half and serve immediately or wrap for later.

NUTRITION INFORMATION PER SERVING
Calories: 350 | Protein: 30g | Fat: 15g | Carbs: 25g

CHICKPEA & CUCUMBER SALAD

INGREDIENTS
- 1 can (15 oz) chickpeas, drained and rinsed
- 1 small cucumber, diced
- ½ cup cherry tomatoes, halved
- ¼ red onion, finely chopped
- 2 tbsp olive oil
- 1 tbsp lemon juice
- ½ tsp salt and pepper
- 1 tbsp chopped parsley

Prep Time: 10 Min
Cook Time: 0 Min

Servings: 2

DIRECTIONS
1. In a large bowl, combine chickpeas, cucumber, cherry tomatoes, and red onion.
2. Drizzle with olive oil and lemon juice, then season with salt and pepper.
3. Toss well to coat all ingredients evenly.
4. Garnish with chopped parsley and serve immediately.

NUTRITION INFORMATION PER SERVING
Calories: 280 | Protein: 12g | Fat: 10g | Carbs: 38g

QUICK CAPRESE SALAD

INGREDIENTS
- 1 cup cherry tomatoes, halved
- 4 oz fresh mozzarella, sliced
- ¼ cup fresh basil leaves
- 1 tbsp olive oil
- 1 tbsp balsamic vinegar
- ¼ tsp salt and pepper

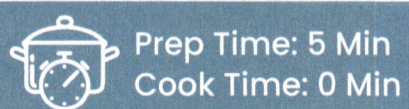 Prep Time: 5 Min
Cook Time: 0 Min

 Servings: 2

DIRECTIONS
1. Arrange cherry tomatoes, mozzarella slices, and basil leaves on a plate.
2. Drizzle with olive oil and balsamic vinegar.
3. Sprinkle with salt and pepper to taste.
4. Serve immediately or refrigerate until ready to eat.

NUTRITION INFORMATION PER SERVING
Calories: 250 | Protein: 15g | Fat: 16g | Carbs: 10g

GREEK YOGURT CHICKEN SALAD

INGREDIENTS

- 1 cup cooked chicken breast, shredded
- ½ cup Greek yogurt
- ½ tsp Dijon mustard
- 1 tbsp lemon juice
- ¼ cup diced celery
- ¼ cup chopped apples
- ¼ tsp salt and pepper

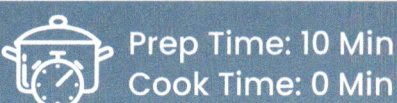 Prep Time: 10 Min
Cook Time: 0 Min

 Servings: 2

DIRECTIONS

1. In a large bowl, mix Greek yogurt, Dijon mustard, and lemon juice.
2. Add shredded chicken, celery, and apples.
3. Stir well to coat all ingredients evenly.
4. Season with salt and pepper to taste.
5. Serve on lettuce leaves, in a sandwich, or as is.

NUTRITION INFORMATION PER SERVING

PAGE | 35 | Calories: 210 | Protein: 28g | Fat: 5g | Carbs: 12g

HUMMUS & VEGGIE WRAP

INGREDIENTS
- 1 whole wheat tortilla
- 3 tbsp hummus
- ¼ cup shredded carrots
- ¼ cup sliced bell peppers
- ¼ cup baby spinach
- ½ chopped avocado
- 1 tbsp crumbled feta cheese (optional)

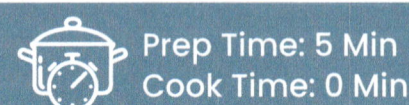 Prep Time: 5 Min
Cook Time: 0 Min

 Servings: 1

DIRECTIONS
1. Spread hummus evenly over the tortilla.
2. Layer shredded carrots, bell peppers, chopped avocado, and baby spinach on top.
3. Sprinkle with crumbled feta cheese if using.
4. Roll the tortilla tightly and slice in half before serving.

NUTRITION INFORMATION PER SERVING

Calories: 280 | Protein: 9g | Fat: 10g | Carbs: 35g

CANNED SALMON & AVOCADO TOAST

INGREDIENTS
- 1 slice whole grain bread
- ½ small avocado, mashed
- 1 can (3 oz) salmon, drained
- ½ tsp lemon juice
- ¼ tsp salt and pepper

Prep Time: 5 Min
Cook Time: 0 Min

Servings: 1

DIRECTIONS
1. Toast the whole grain bread until crispy.
2. Spread mashed avocado evenly over the toast.
3. Top with drained canned salmon.
4. Drizzle with lemon juice and season with salt and pepper.
5. Serve immediately.

NUTRITION INFORMATION PER SERVING
Calories: 320 | Protein: 25g | Fat: 15g | Carbs: 28g

SIMPLE EGG SALAD SANDWICH

INGREDIENTS
- 4 hard-boiled eggs, chopped
- 2 tbsp Greek yogurt or mayonnaise
- ½ tsp Dijon mustard
- ¼ tsp salt and pepper
- 2 slices whole wheat bread

Prep Time: 10 Min
Cook Time: 0 Min
Servings: 2

DIRECTIONS
1. In a bowl, mix chopped eggs, Greek yogurt (or mayonnaise), and Dijon mustard.
2. Season with salt and pepper.
3. Spread egg salad onto one slice of bread and top with the second slice.
4. Slice in half and serve.

NUTRITION INFORMATION PER SERVING
Calories: 290 | Protein: 20g | Fat: 15g | Carbs: 22g

SPICY BLACK BEAN & CHEESE QUESADILLA

INGREDIENTS

- 2 whole wheat tortillas
- ½ cup black beans, drained and rinsed
- ½ cup shredded cheddar cheese
- ¼ tsp chili powder
- ¼ tsp garlic powder
- ¼ cup salsa (for serving)

Prep Time: 5 Min
Cook Time: 10 Min

Servings: 2

DIRECTIONS

1. Heat a non-stick skillet over medium heat.
2. In a bowl, mash the black beans slightly and mix in chili powder and garlic powder.
3. Place one tortilla on the skillet and spread the bean mixture evenly over half of it.
4. Sprinkle shredded cheese over the beans and fold the tortilla in half.
5. Cook for 2–3 minutes per side, until golden brown and the cheese is melted.
6. Remove from the skillet, cut into wedges, and serve with salsa.

NUTRITION INFORMATION PER SERVING

Calories: 310 | Protein: 12g | Fat: 10g | Carbs: 40g

QUICK PITA POCKET WITH CHICKEN & VEGGIES

INGREDIENTS
- 1 whole wheat pita, cut in half
- 1 cup cooked chicken breast, diced
- ½ cup chopped cucumber
- ½ cup cherry tomatoes, halved
- 2 tbsp hummus
- 1 tbsp lemon juice
- ¼ tsp salt and pepper

Prep Time: 10 Min
Cook Time: 0 Min
Servings: 2

DIRECTIONS
1. In a bowl, mix the diced chicken, cucumber, cherry tomatoes, lemon juice, salt, and pepper.
2. Spread hummus inside each pita half.
3. Stuff the pita pockets with the chicken and veggie mixture.
4. Serve immediately or wrap for later.

NUTRITION INFORMATION PER SERVING
Calories: 320 | Protein: 30g | Fat: 7g | Carbs: 35g

QUICK & EASY CUCUMBER YOGURT SALAD

INGREDIENTS
- 1 large cucumber, sliced
- ½ cup Greek yogurt
- 1 tbsp lemon juice
- ½ tsp dried dill
- ¼ tsp salt and pepper

Prep Time: 5 Min
Cook Time: 0 Min

Servings: 2

DIRECTIONS
1. In a mixing bowl, combine the sliced cucumbers, Greek yogurt, lemon juice, and dill.
2. Stir well to coat the cucumbers evenly.
3. Season with salt and pepper to taste.
4. Serve chilled for a refreshing side or light meal.

NUTRITION INFORMATION PER SERVING
Calories: 100 | Protein: 6g | Fat: 2g | Carbs: 15g

CHICKEN & RICE BOWL

INGREDIENTS
- 1 cup cooked brown rice
- 1 cup cooked chicken breast, diced
- ½ cup frozen peas
- 1 tbsp soy sauce
- 1 tsp sesame oil

Prep Time: 5 Min
Cook Time: 10 Min

Servings: 2

DIRECTIONS
1. Heat a pan over medium heat and add the chicken and peas.
2. Stir-fry for 3-4 minutes, until the peas are warmed through.
3. Add the cooked rice, soy sauce, and sesame oil, stirring to combine.
4. Cook for another 2-3 minutes, then serve hot.

NUTRITION INFORMATION PER SERVING
Calories: 350 | Protein: 30g | Fat: 8g | Carbs: 40g

SMOKED SALMON & CREAM CHEESE BAGEL

INGREDIENTS

- 1 whole wheat bagel, sliced in half
- 2 tbsp cream cheese
- 2 oz smoked salmon
- 2 slices tomato
- 2 slices cucumber
- ¼ tsp black pepper

Prep Time: 5 Min
Cook Time: 0 Min

Servings: 1

DIRECTIONS

1. Toast the bagel halves lightly (optional).
2. Spread cream cheese evenly on each half.
3. Layer smoked salmon, tomato slices, and cucumber on one half of the bagel.
4. Sprinkle with black pepper and top with the second bagel half.
5. Serve immediately.

NUTRITION INFORMATION PER SERVING

Calories: 400 | Protein: 22g | Fat: 14g | Carbs: 45g

EGG & AVOCADO ENGLISH MUFFIN

INGREDIENTS
- 1 whole wheat English muffin, split and toasted
- 1 hard-boiled egg, sliced
- ½ small avocado, mashed
- ¼ tsp salt and pepper

Prep Time: 5 Min
Cook Time: 5 Min

Servings: 1

DIRECTIONS
1. Toast the English muffin halves.
2. Spread mashed avocado evenly over each half.
3. Place sliced egg on top and season with salt and pepper.
4. Serve immediately.

NUTRITION INFORMATION PER SERVING
Calories: 280 | Protein: 12g | Fat: 15g | Carbs: 30g

CAPRESE AVOCADO TOAST

INGREDIENTS
- 1 slice whole grain bread
- ½ small avocado, mashed
- 2 slices fresh mozzarella
- 2 cherry tomatoes, sliced
- 1 tsp balsamic glaze

Prep Time: 5 Min
Cook Time: 0 Min

Servings: 1

DIRECTIONS
1. Toast the whole grain bread.
2. Spread mashed avocado evenly on top.
3. Layer mozzarella slices and cherry tomato slices over the avocado.
4. Drizzle with balsamic glaze and serve.

NUTRITION INFORMATION PER SERVING
Calories: 320 | Protein: 12g | Fat: 18g | Carbs: 30g

COTTAGE CHEESE & PINEAPPLE BOWL

INGREDIENTS

- ½ cup cottage cheese
- ½ cup pineapple chunks
- 1 tsp honey (optional)

Prep Time: 5 Min
Cook Time: 0 Min

Servings: 1

DIRECTIONS

1. In a bowl, combine cottage cheese and pineapple chunks.
2. Drizzle with honey if desired.
3. Serve immediately as a refreshing, protein-packed snack.

NUTRITION INFORMATION PER SERVING

Calories: 180 | Protein: 14g | Fat: 3g | Carbs: 25g

QUICK ASIAN-INSPIRED CHICKEN WRAP

INGREDIENTS
- 1 whole wheat tortilla
- ½ cup cooked chicken breast, shredded
- 1 tbsp soy sauce
- ½ cup shredded cabbage
- 1 tbsp sesame seeds

Prep Time: 5 Min
Cook Time: 0 Min

Servings: 1

DIRECTIONS
1. In a bowl, toss shredded chicken with soy sauce.
2. Place cabbage and chicken mixture onto the tortilla.
3. Sprinkle with sesame seeds.
4. Roll the tortilla tightly and serve.

NUTRITION INFORMATION PER SERVING

Calories: 310 | Protein: 28g | Fat: 8g | Carbs: 35g

QUICK ITALIAN TUNA SALAD

INGREDIENTS
- 1 can (5 oz) tuna, drained
- ½ cup cherry tomatoes, halved
- ¼ cup black olives, sliced
- 1 tbsp olive oil
- ½ tsp dried oregano

Prep Time: 5 Min
Cook Time: 0 Min

Servings: 2

DIRECTIONS
1. In a bowl, mix the tuna, cherry tomatoes, and black olives.
2. Drizzle with olive oil and sprinkle with oregano.
3. Stir to combine and serve immediately.

NUTRITION INFORMATION PER SERVING
Calories: 250 | Protein: 30g | Fat: 12g | Carbs: 10g

GARLIC BUTTER SHRIMP & ZOODLES

INGREDIENTS
- 2 cups zucchini noodles (zoodles)
- ½ lb shrimp, peeled and deveined
- 1 tbsp butter
- 2 cloves garlic, minced
- ¼ tsp red pepper flakes
- ½ lemon, juiced
- ¼ tsp salt and pepper

Prep Time: 5 Min
Cook Time: 10 Min

Servings: 2

DIRECTIONS
1. Heat a skillet over medium heat and melt the butter.
2. Add the minced garlic and red pepper flakes, cooking for about 30 seconds until fragrant.
3. Toss in the shrimp and cook for 2-3 minutes per side until pink and opaque.
4. Add the zucchini noodles to the skillet, season with salt and pepper, and stir to combine.
5. Squeeze fresh lemon juice over the dish and cook for another 1-2 minutes, just until the zoodles are slightly softened but not mushy.
6. Serve immediately, garnished with extra lemon if desired.

NUTRITION INFORMATION PER SERVING
Calories: 230 | Protein: 30g | Fat: 8g | Carbs: 10g

CHEESY TURKEY & SPINACH SKILLET

INGREDIENTS

- ½ lb ground turkey
- 1 cup fresh spinach
- ½ cup shredded mozzarella cheese
- ½ tsp garlic powder
- ½ tsp onion powder
- ¼ tsp salt and pepper

Prep Time: 5 Min
Cook Time: 10 Min

Servings: 2

DIRECTIONS

1. Heat a skillet over medium heat and cook the ground turkey, breaking it up as it browns.
2. Once the turkey is fully cooked, add the spinach and cook for another 1-2 minutes until wilted.
3. Season with garlic powder, onion powder, salt, and pepper, stirring to mix.
4. Sprinkle mozzarella cheese on top, cover the skillet, and let the cheese melt for about 2 minutes.
5. Serve hot, straight from the skillet.

NUTRITION INFORMATION PER SERVING

Calories: 320 | Protein: 40g | Fat: 12g | Carbs: 5g

ONE-PAN LEMON GARLIC CHICKEN & BROCCOLI

INGREDIENTS
- 2 boneless, skinless chicken breasts
- 2 cups broccoli florets
- 1 tbsp olive oil
- 2 cloves garlic, minced
- ½ lemon, juiced
- ¼ tsp salt and pepper

Prep Time: 5 Min
Cook Time: 15 Min

Servings: 2

DIRECTIONS
1. Heat olive oil in a large pan over medium heat.
2. Season the chicken breasts with salt and pepper, then add them to the pan.
3. Cook for 4-5 minutes per side until golden brown and cooked through. Remove and set aside.
4. In the same pan, add garlic and broccoli. Sauté for 3-4 minutes until the broccoli is tender.
5. Squeeze fresh lemon juice over everything and return the chicken to the pan.
6. Serve hot, sliced chicken over the broccoli.

NUTRITION INFORMATION PER SERVING
Calories: 340 | Protein: 45g | Fat: 12g | Carbs: 8g

TURKEY AND AVOCADO LETTUCE WRAPS

INGREDIENTS
- 1/2 lb ground turkey
- 1 avocado, sliced
- 1/4 cup red onion, thinly sliced
- 4 large Romaine lettuce leaves
- 1 tsp cumin
- Salt and pepper to taste

Prep Time: 10 Min
Cook Time: 5 Min
Servings: 2

DIRECTIONS
1. Heat a non-stick skillet over medium heat.
2. Add ground turkey and cook until browned, breaking it up into crumbles as it cooks.
3. Season with cumin, salt, and pepper.
4. Remove from heat and set aside.
5. To assemble, place the cooked turkey on the Romaine leaves.
6. Top with avocado slices and red onion.
7. Roll up the lettuce and serve immediately.

NUTRITION INFORMATION PER SERVING
Calories: 320 | Protein: 28g | Fat: 18g | Carbs: 12g

VEGGIE AND HUMMUS WRAP

INGREDIENTS
- 4 whole-wheat tortillas
- 1/2 cup hummus
- 1/2 cucumber, sliced
- 1/2 red bell pepper, sliced
- 1/4 cup shredded carrots
- 1/2 cup spinach leaves

Prep Time: 5 Min
Cook Time: 5 Min

Servings: 2

DIRECTIONS
1. Lay out the tortillas on a flat surface.
2. Spread hummus evenly on each tortilla.
3. Layer with cucumber, bell pepper, shredded carrots, and spinach.
4. Roll up the tortillas and slice them in half.
5. Serve immediately as a quick, refreshing meal.

NUTRITION INFORMATION PER SERVING
Calories: 280 | Protein: 8g | Fat: 14g | Carbs: 35g

TOMATO BASIL MOZZARELLA SKEWERS

INGREDIENTS
- 8 cherry tomatoes
- 8 small mozzarella balls
- 1/4 cup fresh basil leaves
- 1 tbsp balsamic glaze
- Salt and pepper to taste

Prep Time: 5 Min
Cook Time: 0 Min

Servings: 2

DIRECTIONS
1. Thread cherry tomatoes, mozzarella balls, and basil leaves onto small skewers or toothpicks.
2. Drizzle with balsamic glaze and season with salt and pepper.
3. Serve immediately as a fresh and light appetizer.

NUTRITION INFORMATION PER SERVING
Calories: 250 | Protein: 14g | Fat: 16g | Carbs: 8g

AVOCADO & TOMATO TOAST

INGREDIENTS

- 1 slice whole-grain bread
- 1/2 avocado, mashed
- 1/4 cup cherry tomatoes, halved
- 1 tsp olive oil
- Salt and pepper to taste
- Red pepper flakes (optional)

Prep Time: 5 Min
Cook Time: 5 Min

Servings: 1

DIRECTIONS

1. Toast the bread in a toaster or on a skillet.
2. While the bread is toasting, mash the avocado in a small bowl.
3. Spread the mashed avocado on the toasted bread.
4. Top with halved cherry tomatoes, a drizzle of olive oil, salt, pepper, and red pepper flakes.
5. Serve immediately.

NUTRITION INFORMATION PER SERVING

Calories: 230 | Protein: 5g | Fat: 18g | Carbs: 20g

GREEK YOGURT PARFAIT

INGREDIENTS
- 1 cup Greek yogurt
- 1/4 cup granola
- 1/4 cup mixed berries (blueberries, strawberries, raspberries)
- 1 tbsp honey

Prep Time: 5 Min
Cook Time: 0 Min

Servings: 1

DIRECTIONS
1. In a glass or bowl, layer Greek yogurt, granola, and mixed berries.
2. Drizzle with honey.
3. Serve immediately for a quick, balanced breakfast.

NUTRITION INFORMATION PER SERVING

Calories: 290 | Protein: 16g | Fat: 10g | Carbs: 30g

SCRAMBLED EGGS WITH VEGGIES

Prep Time: 5 Min
Cook Time: 5 Min

Servings: 1

INGREDIENTS
- 2 large eggs
- 1/4 cup bell pepper, diced
- 1/4 cup spinach, chopped
- 1 tbsp butter or olive oil
- Salt and pepper to taste

DIRECTIONS
1. Heat butter or olive oil in a skillet over medium heat.
2. Add the diced bell pepper and cook for 1-2 minutes until soft.
3. Add spinach and cook for another 1-2 minutes until wilted.
4. In a bowl, whisk the eggs and pour them into the skillet.
5. Scramble the eggs and vegetables together for 3-4 minutes, until cooked through.
6. Season with salt and pepper, and serve hot.

NUTRITION INFORMATION PER SERVING

Calories: 280 | Protein: 18g | Fat: 22g | Carbs: 6g

MEDITERRANEAN HUMMUS & VEGGIE WRAP

INGREDIENTS
- 1 whole-wheat tortilla
- 1/4 cup hummus
- 1/4 cucumber, sliced
- 1/4 red onion, thinly sliced
- 1/4 cup cherry tomatoes, halved
- Handful of spinach
- Salt and pepper to taste

Prep Time: 10 Min
Cook Time: 0 Min

Servings: 1

DIRECTIONS
1. Spread hummus evenly over the tortilla.
2. Layer cucumber, red onion, cherry tomatoes, and spinach on top of the hummus.
3. Season with salt and pepper.
4. Roll up the tortilla and serve immediately.

NUTRITION INFORMATION PER SERVING
Calories: 320 | Protein: 8g | Fat: 15g | Carbs: 35g

QUICK VEGETABLE STIR-FRY

INGREDIENTS
- 1 cup mixed vegetables (broccoli, carrots, bell peppers)
- 1/2 cup cooked rice or noodles
- 2 tbsp soy sauce
- 1 tbsp sesame oil
- 1 tsp sesame seeds (optional)

Prep Time: 5 Min
Cook Time: 10 Min

Servings: 2

DIRECTIONS
1. Heat sesame oil in a large skillet over medium heat.
2. Add the mixed vegetables and stir-fry for 5-7 minutes, until tender-crisp.
3. Add cooked rice or noodles and soy sauce, stirring to combine.
4. Sprinkle with sesame seeds and serve immediately.

NUTRITION INFORMATION PER SERVING
Calories: 320 | Protein: 7g | Fat: 12g | Carbs: 45g

SIMPLE TUNA SALAD

INGREDIENTS
- 1 can tuna in water, drained
- 1/4 cup mayonnaise
- 1 tbsp mustard
- 1/4 cup chopped celery
- Salt and pepper to taste

Prep Time: 5 Min
Cook Time: 0 Min

Servings: 2

DIRECTIONS
1. In a bowl, mix together the tuna, mayonnaise, mustard, and celery.
2. Season with salt and pepper to taste.
3. Serve on a bed of lettuce or in a sandwich, if desired.

NUTRITION INFORMATION PER SERVING
Calories: 210 | Protein: 28g | Fat: 10g | Carbs: 2g

AVOCADO & BLACK BEAN SALAD

INGREDIENTS
- 1 avocado, diced
- 1 can black beans, drained and rinsed
- 1/4 cup red onion, finely chopped
- 1/4 cup cilantro, chopped
- Juice of 1 lime
- Salt and pepper to taste

Prep Time: 10 Min
Cook Time: 0 Min

Servings: 2

DIRECTIONS
1. In a bowl, combine diced avocado, black beans, red onion, and cilantro.
2. Squeeze lime juice over the salad and toss gently.
3. Season with salt and pepper, and serve immediately.

NUTRITION INFORMATION PER SERVING
Calories: 280 | Protein: 8g | Fat: 18g | Carbs: 30g

QUINOA VEGGIE STIR-FRY

INGREDIENTS
- 1 cup cooked quinoa
- 1/2 cup bell pepper, diced
- 1/2 cup zucchini, diced
- 1 tbsp soy sauce
- 1 tbsp olive oil

Prep Time: 5 Min
Cook Time: 10 Min

Servings: 2

DIRECTIONS
1. Heat olive oil in a skillet over medium heat.
2. Add diced bell pepper and zucchini, and cook for 3-4 minutes until tender.
3. Stir in cooked quinoa and soy sauce, and cook for an additional 2-3 minutes.
4. Serve hot.

NUTRITION INFORMATION PER SERVING

Calories: 250 | Protein: 7g | Fat: 10g | Carbs: 35g

GARLIC & HERB SHRIMP SKILLET

INGREDIENTS

- 1 lb shrimp, peeled and deveined
- 2 tbsp olive oil
- 2 garlic cloves, minced
- 1 tsp dried oregano
- 1 tsp paprika
- Salt and pepper to taste

Prep Time: 5 Min
Cook Time: 10 Min

Servings: 2

DIRECTIONS

1. Heat olive oil in a skillet over medium-high heat.
2. Add minced garlic and sauté for 1 minute until fragrant.
3. Add shrimp, oregano, paprika, salt, and pepper.
4. Cook for 3-4 minutes on each side until shrimp are pink and opaque.
5. Serve with rice or a side salad.

NUTRITION INFORMATION PER SERVING

Calories: 250 | Protein: 25g | Fat: 15g | Carbs: 4g

30-MINUTE MEALS

SPINACH & FETA OMELET

INGREDIENTS

- 2 large eggs
- 1/4 cup feta cheese, crumbled
- 1/2 cup fresh spinach, chopped
- 1 tbsp olive oil
- Salt and pepper to taste

Prep Time: 5 Min
Cook Time: 10 Min

Servings: 1

DIRECTIONS

1. Heat olive oil in a non-stick skillet over medium heat.
2. Add spinach and sauté for 1-2 minutes until wilted.
3. In a bowl, whisk the eggs with salt and pepper.
4. Pour the eggs into the skillet over the cooked spinach.
5. Sprinkle feta cheese evenly on top of the eggs.
6. Allow eggs to cook for about 3-4 minutes, or until the edges start to set.
7. Carefully fold the omelet in half and cook for an additional 1-2 minutes.
8. Serve immediately with your choice of toast or a side salad.

NUTRITION INFORMATION PER SERVING

Calories: 280 | Protein: 20g | Fat: 20g | Carbs: 3g

BANANA PANCAKES

INGREDIENTS

- 1 ripe banana
- 2 large eggs
- 1/4 tsp baking powder
- Pinch of cinnamon
- 1 tbsp butter, for cooking

Prep Time: 5 Min
Cook Time: 10 Min

Servings: 2

DIRECTIONS

1. In a bowl, mash the banana until smooth.
2. Whisk in the eggs, baking powder, and cinnamon until fully combined.
3. Heat a skillet over medium heat and add butter.
4. Pour small dollops of batter into the skillet to form pancakes.
5. Cook for 2-3 minutes on each side until golden brown.
6. Serve hot with maple syrup, fruit, or a dollop of yogurt.

NUTRITION INFORMATION PER SERVING

Calories: 220 | Protein: 8g | Fat: 14g | Carbs: 22g

BREAKFAST SKILLET WITH SAUSAGE & POTATOES

INGREDIENTS

- 1 sausage link (or 1/2 cup ground sausage)
- 2 small potatoes, diced
- 1/4 onion, chopped
- 1/4 cup shredded cheddar cheese (optional)
- 1 tbsp olive oil
- Salt and pepper to taste

Prep Time: 10 Min
Cook Time: 15 Min

Servings: 2

DIRECTIONS

1. Heat olive oil in a large skillet over medium heat.
2. Add diced potatoes and cook for 8-10 minutes, stirring occasionally, until golden and tender.
3. While potatoes are cooking, crumble the sausage into the pan and cook until browned, about 5 minutes.
4. Add the chopped onion to the pan and cook for another 2-3 minutes, until softened.
5. Season with salt and pepper, and sprinkle with cheese if desired.
6. Serve hot with a side of fruit or toast.

NUTRITION INFORMATION PER SERVING

Calories: 400 | Protein: 18g | Fat: 25g | Carbs: 28g

QUINOA & CHICKPEA SALAD BOWL

INGREDIENTS
- 1 cup cooked quinoa
- 1/2 cup canned chickpeas, drained and rinsed
- 1/2 cucumber, diced
- 1/4 red onion, thinly sliced
- 1 tbsp olive oil
- Juice of 1 lemon
- Salt and pepper to taste

Prep Time: 10 Min
Cook Time: 15 Min
Servings: 2

DIRECTIONS
1. In a large bowl, combine cooked quinoa, chickpeas, cucumber, and red onion.
2. Drizzle olive oil and lemon juice over the ingredients.
3. Toss everything together until well mixed.
4. Season with salt and pepper, then refrigerate for 10-15 minutes before serving.
5. Serve chilled or at room temperature.

NUTRITION INFORMATION PER SERVING
Calories: 320 | Protein: 10g | Fat: 15g | Carbs: 35g

SWEET POTATO & BLACK BEAN CHILI

INGREDIENTS
- 1 large sweet potato, peeled and diced
- 1 can black beans, drained and rinsed
- 1 can diced tomatoes (14 oz)
- 1 tbsp chili powder
- 1/2 tsp garlic powder
- 1/2 onion, chopped
- 1 tbsp olive oil
- Salt and pepper to taste

Prep Time: 5 Min
Cook Time: 25 Min

Servings: 3

DIRECTIONS
1. Heat olive oil in a large pot over medium heat.
2. Add chopped onion and sauté for 2-3 minutes until softened.
3. Add diced sweet potato, black beans, and tomatoes to the pot.
4. Stir in chili powder, garlic powder, salt, and pepper.
5. Cover and simmer for 20 minutes, or until the sweet potato is tender.
6. Serve hot with a sprinkle of cilantro or a dollop of sour cream.

NUTRITION INFORMATION PER SERVING
Calories: 280 | Protein: 9g | Fat: 5g | Carbs: 50g

LENTIL SOUP WITH SPINACH

INGREDIENTS
- 1 cup dry lentils
- 4 cups vegetable broth
- 1 cup spinach, chopped
- 1 carrot, peeled and diced
- 1 tbsp olive oil
- Salt and pepper to taste

Prep Time: 5 Min
Cook Time: 25 Min

Servings: 3

DIRECTIONS
1. Heat olive oil in a large pot over medium heat.
2. Add diced carrot and sauté for 3-4 minutes until softened.
3. Add lentils and vegetable broth, bring to a boil.
4. Reduce heat and simmer for 20 minutes, or until lentils are tender.
5. Stir in chopped spinach and cook for an additional 2 minutes.
6. Season with salt and pepper and serve hot.

NUTRITION INFORMATION PER SERVING

Calories: 230 | Protein: 15g | Fat: 4g | Carbs: 38g

BAKED LEMON HERB CHICKEN

INGREDIENTS
- 2 chicken breasts
- Zest of 1 lemon
- 1 tsp garlic powder
- 1 tsp dried thyme
- 1 tbsp olive oil
- Salt and pepper to taste

Prep Time: 5 Min
Cook Time: 25 Min

Servings: 2

DIRECTIONS
1. Preheat the oven to 375°F (190°C).
2. Rub the chicken breasts with olive oil, lemon zest, garlic powder, thyme, salt, and pepper.
3. Place the chicken breasts on a baking sheet and bake for 20-25 minutes until cooked through.
4. Serve with a side of roasted vegetables or a fresh salad.

NUTRITION INFORMATION PER SERVING
Calories: 230 | Protein: 40g | Fat: 10g | Carbs: 2g

SALMON WITH ROASTED VEGETABLES

INGREDIENTS
- 2 salmon fillets
- 1 zucchini, sliced
- 1 bell pepper, sliced
- 1 tbsp olive oil
- Salt and pepper to taste

Prep Time: 10 Min
Cook Time: 20 Min

Servings: 2

DIRECTIONS
1. Preheat the oven to 400°F (200°C).
2. Toss the zucchini and bell pepper in olive oil, salt, and pepper.
3. Place the salmon fillets and vegetables on a baking sheet.
4. Roast for 15-20 minutes, or until the salmon is cooked through and vegetables are tender.
5. Serve with a squeeze of lemon juice and a sprinkle of fresh herbs.

NUTRITION INFORMATION PER SERVING
Calories: 350 | Protein: 30g | Fat: 22g | Carbs: 15g

PESTO CHICKEN SALAD

INGREDIENTS

- 2 chicken breasts, cooked and shredded
- 1/2 cup pesto
- 1/2 cup cherry tomatoes, halved
- 1/4 cup red onion, thinly sliced
- 1 cup mixed greens

Prep Time: 10 Min
Cook Time: 10 Min

Servings: 2

DIRECTIONS

1. Toss the shredded chicken with pesto until evenly coated.
2. Add cherry tomatoes, red onion, and mixed greens.
3. Toss again to combine.
4. Serve the salad in bowls, with extra pesto for drizzling if desired.

NUTRITION INFORMATION PER SERVING

Calories: 350 | Protein: 35g | Fat: 22g | Carbs: 8g

LEMON HERB ROASTED CHICKEN BREASTS

INGREDIENTS
- 2 chicken breasts
- 1 tbsp olive oil
- Juice of 1 lemon
- 1 tsp dried thyme
- 1 tsp garlic powder
- Salt and pepper to taste

Prep Time: 10 Min
Cook Time: 20 Min

Servings: 2

DIRECTIONS
1. Preheat the oven to 400°F (200°C).
2. Rub the chicken breasts with olive oil, lemon juice, thyme, garlic powder, salt, and pepper.
3. Place the chicken on a baking sheet and bake for 18-20 minutes, until cooked through.
4. Serve with roasted vegetables or a simple salad.

NUTRITION INFORMATION PER SERVING
Calories: 290 | Protein: 40g | Fat: 14g | Carbs: 2g

ONE-PAN BAKED SALMON WITH VEGGIES

INGREDIENTS

- 2 salmon fillets
- 1 tbsp olive oil
- 1 lemon, sliced
- 1 cup baby carrots
- 1 cup broccoli florets
- Salt and pepper to taste

Prep Time: 5 Min
Cook Time: 20 Min

Servings: 2

DIRECTIONS

1. Preheat the oven to 375°F (190°C).
2. Place the salmon fillets on a baking sheet, drizzle with olive oil, and season with salt and pepper.
3. Arrange lemon slices around the salmon, and place baby carrots and broccoli florets around the fillets.
4. Bake for 15-20 minutes, until salmon is cooked through and veggies are tender.
5. Serve immediately.

NUTRITION INFORMATION PER SERVING
Calories: 350 | Protein: 35g | Fat: 20g | Carbs: 15g

SWEET POTATO & BLACK BEAN TACOS

INGREDIENTS
- 2 small sweet potatoes, peeled and diced
- 1 can black beans, drained and rinsed
- 1 tbsp olive oil
- 1 tsp chili powder
- 1/2 tsp cumin
- 4 small tortillas
- Salsa (optional)
- Cilantro (optional)

Prep Time: 10 Min
Cook Time: 10 Min

Servings: 2

DIRECTIONS
1. Heat olive oil in a skillet over medium heat.
2. Add diced sweet potatoes and cook for 8-10 minutes until tender.
3. Stir in black beans, chili powder, and cumin. Cook for another 2 minutes until heated through.
4. Warm the tortillas in the microwave or on a skillet.
5. Fill the tortillas with the sweet potato and black bean mixture.
6. Top with salsa and cilantro, if desired, and serve.

NUTRITION INFORMATION PER SERVING
Calories: 320 | Protein: 10g | Fat: 12g | Carbs: 40g

QUICK BEEF STIR-FRY

INGREDIENTS
- 1/2 lb beef (sirloin or flank steak), thinly sliced
- 1 tbsp soy sauce
- 1 tbsp oyster sauce
- 2 cups broccoli florets
- 1/2 bell pepper, sliced
- 1/2 onion, sliced
- 1 tbsp olive oil
- Cooked rice (for serving)

Prep Time: 10 Min
Cook Time: 10 Min

Servings: 2

DIRECTIONS
1. Heat olive oil in a skillet or wok over medium-high heat.
2. Add the beef and stir-fry for 2-3 minutes until browned.
3. Add the bell pepper, broccoli and onion and cook for an additional 2-3 minutes.
4. Stir in the soy sauce and oyster sauce and cook for another 2 minutes.
5. Serve over cooked rice.

NUTRITION INFORMATION PER SERVING
Calories: 350 | Protein: 30g | Fat: 20g | Carbs: 10g

LEMON GARLIC SHRIMP PASTA

INGREDIENTS

- 1/2 lb shrimp, peeled and deveined
- 4 oz spaghetti (or gluten-free pasta)
- 2 garlic cloves, minced
- 1 tbsp olive oil
- Juice of 1 lemon
- 1/4 cup parsley, chopped

Prep Time: 10 Min
Cook Time: 10 Min

Servings: 2

DIRECTIONS

1. Cook the pasta according to package instructions, drain, and set aside.
2. Heat olive oil in a skillet over medium heat.
3. Add the garlic and shrimp and cook for 2-3 minutes until shrimp are pink and opaque.
4. Add the cooked pasta, lemon juice, and parsley to the skillet, and toss to combine.
5. Serve immediately.

NUTRITION INFORMATION PER SERVING

Calories: 380 | Protein: 30g | Fat: 14g | Carbs: 35g

SPICY CHICKEN & VEGGIE SKILLET

INGREDIENTS
- 2 chicken breasts, slices
- 1/2 red bell pepper, diced
- 1/2 zucchini, diced
- 1 tbsp olive oil
- 1 tsp paprika
- 1/2 tsp cayenne pepper
- Salt and pepper to taste

Prep Time: 10 Min
Cook Time: 15 Min
Servings: 2

DIRECTIONS
1. Heat olive oil in a large skillet over medium heat.
2. Add chicken slices and cook for 5-6 minutes until browned.
3. Stir in the bell pepper and zucchini, and cook for another 5-6 minutes until tender.
4. Season with paprika, cayenne pepper, salt, and pepper.
5. Serve hot.

NUTRITION INFORMATION PER SERVING
Calories: 280 | Protein: 35g | Fat: 14g | Carbs: 8g

EASY BAKED ZITI

INGREDIENTS

- 8 oz ziti pasta
- 1 cup marinara sauce
- 1 cup shredded mozzarella cheese
- 1/4 cup grated Parmesan cheese
- 1 tsp Italian seasoning

Prep Time: 10 Min
Cook Time: 20 Min

Servings: 4

DIRECTIONS

1. Preheat the oven to 375°F (190°C).
2. Cook the ziti pasta according to package instructions and drain.
3. In a baking dish, combine the pasta with marinara sauce, mozzarella, and Parmesan cheese.
4. Sprinkle with Italian seasoning.
5. Bake for 15-20 minutes, until the cheese is melted and bubbly.
6. Serve immediately.

NUTRITION INFORMATION PER SERVING

Calories: 400 | Protein: 18g | Fat: 18g | Carbs: 40g

CHICKEN CAESAR WRAPS

INGREDIENTS
- 2 chicken breasts, cooked and sliced
- 2 whole-wheat tortillas
- 1/2 cup Caesar dressing
- 1 cup Romaine lettuce, chopped
- 1/4 cup grated Parmesan cheese

Prep Time: 5 Min
Cook Time: 10 Min
Servings: 2

DIRECTIONS
1. In a bowl, toss the sliced chicken with Caesar dressing.
2. Lay the tortillas flat and divide the chicken mixture between them.
3. Top with Romaine lettuce and Parmesan cheese.
4. Roll up the tortillas and serve immediately.

NUTRITION INFORMATION PER SERVING
Calories: 450 | Protein: 35g | Fat: 25g | Carbs: 30g

QUICK VEGGIE STIR-FRY WITH TOFU

INGREDIENTS

- 1 block firm tofu, cubed
- 1 cup broccoli florets
- 1/2 bell pepper, sliced
- 1 small carrot, julienned
- 2 tbsp soy sauce
- 1 tbsp sesame oil
- 1 tbsp hoisin sauce
- 1 tsp grated ginger

Prep Time: 10 Min
Cook Time: 10 Min

Servings: 2

DIRECTIONS

1. Press the tofu to remove excess moisture, then cut into cubes.
2. Heat sesame oil in a skillet over medium heat.
3. Add tofu cubes and cook for 5-7 minutes, until lightly golden.
4. Add the broccoli, bell pepper, and carrot, and stir-fry for another 3-4 minutes.
5. Stir in soy sauce, hoisin sauce, and grated ginger. Cook for another minute until everything is well coated.
6. Serve immediately.

NUTRITION INFORMATION PER SERVING

Calories: 330 | Protein: 20g | Fat: 22g | Carbs: 15g

CHICKEN AND SPINACH ALFREDO

INGREDIENTS
- 2 chicken breasts, sliced
- 2 cups fresh spinach
- 1/2 cup Alfredo sauce
- 4 oz fettuccine pasta
- 1 tbsp olive oil
- Salt and pepper to taste

Prep Time: 5 Min
Cook Time: 15 Min

Servings: 2

DIRECTIONS
1. Cook the fettuccine pasta according to package instructions, then drain and set aside.
2. Heat olive oil in a skillet over medium heat.
3. Add sliced chicken breasts and cook for 5-6 minutes until browned and cooked through.
4. Stir in spinach and cook until wilted, about 2 minutes.
5. Add Alfredo sauce and cooked pasta, stirring to combine.
6. Season with salt and pepper, and serve hot.

NUTRITION INFORMATION PER SERVING
Calories: 420 | Protein: 35g | Fat: 22g | Carbs: 30g

QUICK BAKED TILAPIA WITH LEMON AND GARLIC

INGREDIENTS
- 2 tilapia fillets
- 2 tbsp olive oil
- 1 lemon, sliced
- 2 garlic cloves, minced
- Salt and pepper to taste

Prep Time: 5 Min
Cook Time: 12 Min

Servings: 2

DIRECTIONS
1. Preheat the oven to 400°F (200°C).
2. Place tilapia fillets on a baking sheet lined with parchment paper.
3. Drizzle with olive oil, minced garlic, and season with salt and pepper.
4. Arrange lemon slices over the fish.
5. Bake for 10-12 minutes until the fish flakes easily with a fork.
6. Serve with steamed vegetables or a side salad.

NUTRITION INFORMATION PER SERVING
Calories: 230 | Protein: 35g | Fat: 10g | Carbs: 2g

PESTO CHICKEN WITH ZUCCHINI NOODLES

INGREDIENTS
- 2 chicken breasts
- 2 medium zucchinis, spiralized into noodles
- 1/4 cup pesto sauce
- 1 tbsp olive oil
- Salt and pepper to taste

Prep Time: 10 Min
Cook Time: 10 Min
Servings: 2

DIRECTIONS
1. Heat olive oil in a skillet over medium heat.
2. Season chicken breasts with salt and pepper, then cook in the skillet for 6-7 minutes per side, until golden brown and cooked through.
3. Remove chicken from the skillet and set aside.
4. In the same skillet, add zucchini noodles and sauté for 2-3 minutes until slightly softened.
5. Toss zucchini noodles with pesto sauce.
6. Slice the chicken and serve over the pesto zucchini noodles.

NUTRITION INFORMATION PER SERVING
Calories: 350 | Protein: 35g | Fat: 22g | Carbs: 10g

GARLIC PARMESAN ROASTED SHRIMP

INGREDIENTS

- 1 lb large shrimp, peeled and deveined
- 2 tbsp olive oil
- 2 garlic cloves, minced
- 1/4 cup grated Parmesan cheese
- 1 tbsp parsley, chopped
- Salt and pepper to taste

Prep Time: 5 Min
Cook Time: 10 Min

Servings: 2

DIRECTIONS

1. Preheat the oven to 400°F (200°C).
2. Toss shrimp with olive oil, garlic, salt, and pepper.
3. Spread the shrimp in a single layer on a baking sheet.
4. Sprinkle with Parmesan cheese and bake for 6-8 minutes, until shrimp are pink and cooked through.
5. Garnish with parsley and serve immediately.

NUTRITION INFORMATION PER SERVING

Calories: 310 | Protein: 28g | Fat: 18g | Carbs: 3g

SPICY CHICKPEA AND QUINOA BOWL

INGREDIENTS

- 1 can (15 oz) chickpeas, drained and rinsed
- 1/2 cup quinoa
- 1 tbsp olive oil
- 1 tsp paprika
- 1/2 tsp cayenne pepper
- Salt and pepper to taste
- 1/4 cup Greek yogurt (for topping)
- 1 tbsp fresh cilantro, chopped

Prep Time: 10 Min
Cook Time: 15 Min

Servings: 2

DIRECTIONS

1. Cook the quinoa according to package instructions.
2. While the quinoa cooks, heat olive oil in a skillet over medium heat.
3. Add chickpeas, paprika, cayenne pepper, salt, and pepper to the skillet, and cook for 5-7 minutes until crispy.
4. Serve the chickpeas over the quinoa.
5. Top with Greek yogurt and fresh cilantro for added flavor.

NUTRITION INFORMATION PER SERVING

Calories: 360 | Protein: 14g | Fat: 12g | Carbs: 50g

SIMPLE BEEF AND VEGGIE STIR-FRY

INGREDIENTS
- 1/2 lb lean ground beef
- 1/2 cup bell pepper, sliced
- 1/2 cup mushrooms, sliced
- 1 small zucchini, sliced
- 2 cups broccoli florets
- 2 tbsp soy sauce
- 1 tbsp olive oil
- 1 tsp ginger, grated
- Salt and pepper to taste

Prep Time: 10 Min
Cook Time: 10 Min

Servings: 2

DIRECTIONS
1. Heat olive oil in a large skillet over medium heat.
2. Add ground beef and cook for 5-6 minutes until browned.
3. Add bell pepper, mushrooms, zucchini, broccoli and grated ginger to the skillet, and cook for an additional 3-4 minutes until the veggies soften.
4. Stir in soy sauce, salt, and pepper, and cook for another minute.
5. Serve the stir-fry hot, and enjoy!

NUTRITION INFORMATION PER SERVING
Calories: 300 | Protein: 28g | Fat: 18g | Carbs: 12g

MEDITERRANEAN CHICKEN SKEWERS WITH TZATZIKI

INGREDIENTS

- 2 chicken breasts, cut into cubes
- 1 tbsp olive oil
- 1 tbsp lemon juice
- 1 tsp dried oregano
- Salt and pepper to taste
- 1/4 cup tzatziki sauce (store-bought or homemade)

Prep Time: 10 Min
Cook Time: 12 Min

Servings: 2

DIRECTIONS

1. Preheat the grill or a grill pan over medium-high heat.
2. Toss chicken cubes with olive oil, lemon juice, oregano, salt, and pepper.
3. Thread chicken onto skewers and grill for 5-6 minutes per side until fully cooked.
4. Serve with tzatziki sauce on the side for dipping.

NUTRITION INFORMATION PER SERVING

Calories: 280 | Protein: 38g | Fat: 14g | Carbs: 6g

SPINACH AND CHEESE STUFFED PORTOBELLO MUSHROOMS

INGREDIENTS

- 2 large Portobello mushrooms
- 1 cup fresh spinach
- 1/2 cup ricotta cheese
- 1/4 cup shredded mozzarella cheese
- 1 tbsp olive oil
- Salt and pepper to taste
- 1 tsp garlic powder

Prep Time: 10 Min
Cook Time: 15 Min

Servings: 2

DIRECTIONS

1. Preheat the oven to 375°F (190°C).
2. Remove the stems from the mushrooms and place them on a baking sheet.
3. Heat olive oil in a skillet over medium heat. Add spinach and cook until wilted, about 2-3 minutes.
4. In a bowl, mix cooked spinach with ricotta and mozzarella. Season with salt, pepper, and garlic powder.
5. Stuff the mushroom caps with the spinach and cheese mixture.
6. Bake for 12-15 minutes, until the mushrooms are tender and the cheese is melted.

NUTRITION INFORMATION PER SERVING

Calories: 250 | Protein: 20g | Fat: 16g | Carbs: 12g

QUICK EGG FRIED RICE

INGREDIENTS

- 2 cups cooked rice (preferably day-old)
- 2 eggs, beaten
- 1/2 cup peas and carrots, frozen
- 2 tbsp soy sauce
- 1 tbsp sesame oil
- 1/4 cup green onions, sliced

Prep Time: 5 Min
Cook Time: 10 Min

Servings: 2

DIRECTIONS

1. Heat sesame oil in a large skillet or wok over medium heat.
2. Add the peas and carrots and cook for 2-3 minutes until heated through.
3. Push the veggies to one side of the pan, and scramble the beaten eggs on the other side.
4. Once the eggs are cooked, add the rice and soy sauce.
5. Stir everything together and cook for another 3-4 minutes.
6. Garnish with green onions and serve.

NUTRITION INFORMATION PER SERVING

Calories: 380 | Protein: 12g | Fat: 16g | Carbs: 48g

BAKED CHICKEN THIGHS WITH SWEET POTATOES

INGREDIENTS
- 2 bone-in chicken thighs
- 2 small sweet potatoes, slices
- 1 tbsp olive oil
- 1 tsp paprika
- Salt and pepper to taste

Prep Time: 5 Min
Cook Time: 25 Min

Servings: 2

DIRECTIONS
1. Preheat the oven to 400°F (200°C).
2. Rub chicken thighs with olive oil, paprika, salt, and pepper.
3. Place the chicken thighs on a baking sheet and arrange sweet potato slices around them.
4. Roast in the oven for 25 minutes or until the chicken is cooked through and the sweet potatoes are tender.
5. Serve hot.

NUTRITION INFORMATION PER SERVING
Calories: 450 | Protein: 35g | Fat: 22g | Carbs: 40g

LEMON GARLIC SHRIMP AND ASPARAGUS

INGREDIENTS

- 1/2 lb large shrimp, peeled and deveined
- 1 bunch asparagus, trimmed and cut into 2-inch pieces
- 2 tbsp olive oil
- 2 garlic cloves, minced
- Zest and juice of 1 lemon
- Salt and pepper to taste

Prep Time: 10 Min
Cook Time: 10 Min

Servings: 2

DIRECTIONS

1. Heat olive oil in a large skillet over medium heat.
2. Add minced garlic and cook for 1 minute until fragrant.
3. Add shrimp and cook for 3-4 minutes, until pink.
4. Add asparagus, lemon zest, and lemon juice, and cook for another 4-5 minutes until asparagus is tender.
5. Season with salt and pepper, and serve immediately.

NUTRITION INFORMATION PER SERVING

Calories: 330 | Protein: 28g | Fat: 22g | Carbs: 10g

SAUCES, DRESSINGS & SIMPLE SEASONINGS

SIMPLE TOMATO SAUCE

INGREDIENTS
- 1 can (400g) crushed tomatoes
- 1 tbsp olive oil
- 1 garlic clove, minced
- 1 tsp dried basil
- Salt and pepper to taste

Prep Time: 5 Min
Cook Time: 10 Min

Servings: 4

DIRECTIONS
1. Heat the olive oil in a medium saucepan over medium heat.
2. Once the oil is hot, add the minced garlic and sauté for about 1 minute, or until fragrant. Stir occasionally to avoid burning.
3. Add the can of crushed tomatoes into the saucepan, stirring to combine with the garlic.
4. Season the sauce with dried basil, salt, and pepper. Mix well to ensure the flavors meld.
5. Reduce the heat to low and simmer for about 10 minutes, stirring occasionally. The sauce should thicken slightly. If you prefer a smoother texture, you can use an immersion blender for a few seconds.
6. Taste and adjust the seasoning, adding more salt or pepper if necessary. Serve immediately over pasta, grilled vegetables, or use as a base for pizza.

NUTRITION INFORMATION PER SERVING
Calories: 60 | Protein: 2g | Fat: 3g | Carbs: 8g

CREAMY AVOCADO DRESSING

INGREDIENTS
- 1 ripe avocado
- 2 tbsp Greek yogurt
- 1 tbsp lime juice
- 1 tsp garlic powder
- Salt and pepper to taste

Prep Time: 5 Min
Cook Time: 0 Min

Servings: 4

DIRECTIONS
1. Cut the avocado in half, remove the pit, and scoop out the flesh into a food processor or blender.
2. Add the Greek yogurt, lime juice, and garlic powder into the blender with the avocado.
3. Blend on high until the mixture is smooth and creamy. If the dressing is too thick, add a tablespoon of water or extra lime juice to thin it out to your desired consistency.
4. Taste and season with salt and pepper to your preference.
5. This dressing is perfect for drizzling over salads, grilled chicken, or as a dip for veggies.

NUTRITION INFORMATION PER SERVING
Calories: 90 | Protein: 2g | Fat: 8g | Carbs: 6g

GARLIC BUTTER SAUCE

INGREDIENTS

- 1/4 cup unsalted butter
- 3 garlic cloves, minced
- 1 tbsp fresh parsley, chopped
- Salt to taste

Prep Time: 3 Min
Cook Time: 5 Min

Servings: 4

DIRECTIONS

1. prevent it from browning.
2. Once the butter has melted, add the minced garlic and sauté for about 1-2 minutes, or until the garlic is fragrant and golden. Be careful not to burn the garlic.
3. Stir in the chopped parsley and season with salt to taste.
4. Remove from heat and pour the sauce over your favorite pasta, roasted vegetables, or grilled fish.
5. This rich and savory sauce can also be used to drizzle over steamed vegetables for an extra burst of flavor.

NUTRITION INFORMATION PER SERVING
Calories: 120 | Protein: 1g | Fat: 12g | Carbs: 1g

SWEET AND SPICY STIR-FRY SAUCE

INGREDIENTS
- 2 tbsp soy sauce
- 1 tbsp honey
- 1 tsp chili flakes
- 1 tbsp rice vinegar
- 1 tsp sesame oil

Prep Time: 5 Min
Cook Time: 0 Min
Servings: 4

DIRECTIONS
1. In a small bowl, whisk together the soy sauce, honey, and rice vinegar until the honey dissolves completely.
2. Add the chili flakes for a spicy kick and stir to combine.
3. Drizzle in the sesame oil and whisk until the sauce is smooth and well-blended.
4. Taste and adjust the sweetness or spice level by adding more honey or chili flakes, depending on your preference.
5. Use this versatile sauce over stir-fried vegetables, tofu, or chicken. You can also add it as a topping for rice bowls or grain salads.

NUTRITION INFORMATION PER SERVING
Calories: 45 | Protein: 1g | Fat: 2g | Carbs: 7g

CLASSIC VINAIGRETTE DRESSING

INGREDIENTS
- 3 tbsp olive oil
- 1 tbsp balsamic vinegar
- 1 tsp Dijon mustard
- Salt and pepper to taste

Prep Time: 5 Min
Cook Time: 0 Min

Servings: 6

DIRECTIONS
1. In a small bowl or jar, whisk together the olive oil, balsamic vinegar, and Dijon mustard until the mixture is smooth and slightly emulsified.
2. Season with salt and pepper to taste. If you prefer a stronger mustard flavor, feel free to add an extra teaspoon of Dijon.
3. Pour the vinaigrette over a salad, or use it as a marinade for grilled vegetables or meats.
4. The dressing can be stored in the refrigerator for up to 1 week. Make sure to shake or stir it before each use.

NUTRITION INFORMATION PER SERVING
Calories: 80 | Protein: 0g | Fat: 9g | Carbs: 1g

LEMON HERB DRESSING

INGREDIENTS
- 2 tbsp olive oil
- 1 tbsp lemon juice
- 1 tsp dried oregano
- 1 tsp Dijon mustard
- Salt and pepper to taste

Prep Time: 5 Min
Cook Time: 0 Min

Servings: 4

DIRECTIONS
1. In a small bowl, whisk together the olive oil, lemon juice, and Dijon mustard.
2. Add the dried oregano, salt, and pepper, then whisk until the dressing is smooth and well-combined.
3. Taste and adjust the seasoning if necessary. If you prefer more acidity, add a little extra lemon juice.
4. Pour the dressing over mixed greens, roasted vegetables, or grilled fish. It also works great as a marinade for chicken or tofu.
5. Store any leftovers in an airtight container in the refrigerator for up to 1 week.

NUTRITION INFORMATION PER SERVING
Calories: 90 | Protein: 0g | Fat: 9g | Carbs: 1g

TANGY YOGURT DRESSING

INGREDIENTS
- 1/2 cup plain Greek yogurt
- 1 tbsp lemon juice
- 1 tsp honey
- 1/2 tsp garlic powder
- Salt and pepper to taste

Prep Time: 5 Min
Cook Time: 0 Min

Servings: 4

DIRECTIONS
1. In a small bowl, combine the Greek yogurt, lemon juice, and honey.
2. Add the garlic powder, salt, and pepper, and mix until the dressing is creamy and smooth.
3. Taste and adjust the sweetness or seasoning, depending on your preference. For a thinner consistency, add a little water or extra lemon juice.
4. This creamy yogurt dressing is perfect for drizzling over salads, as a dip for raw vegetables, or even as a topping for baked potatoes.
5. Store any leftovers in the fridge for up to 3 days.

NUTRITION INFORMATION PER SERVING

Calories: 50 | Protein: 4g | Fat: 2g | Carbs: 5g

BASIC PESTO SAUCE

INGREDIENTS
- 1 cup fresh basil leaves
- 1/4 cup olive oil
- 2 tbsp grated Parmesan cheese
- 1 clove garlic
- Salt and pepper to taste

Prep Time: 5 Min
Cook Time: 0 Min

Servings: 4

DIRECTIONS
1. In a food processor or blender, combine the fresh basil, olive oil, Parmesan cheese, and garlic.
2. Pulse until the mixture reaches a smooth paste. Scrape down the sides as needed to ensure everything is well-blended.
3. Season with salt and pepper to taste.
4. This pesto sauce is perfect as a pasta sauce, spread on sandwiches, or drizzled over roasted vegetables.
5. Store any leftovers in an airtight container in the refrigerator for up to 1 week.

NUTRITION INFORMATION PER SERVING
Calories: 150 | Protein: 4g | Fat: 14g | Carbs: 4g

PEANUT BUTTER DIPPING SAUCE

INGREDIENTS
- 1/4 cup peanut butter (smooth or chunky)
- 2 tbsp soy sauce
- 1 tbsp rice vinegar
- 1 tsp honey
- 1/2 tsp chili flakes (optional)

Prep Time: 5 Min
Cook Time: 0 Min

Servings: 4

DIRECTIONS
1. In a small bowl, whisk together the peanut butter, soy sauce, rice vinegar, and honey until smooth.
2. If you like a bit of heat, add the chili flakes and mix well.
3. For a thinner consistency, add a teaspoon of water at a time until you reach your desired texture.
4. This peanut butter dipping sauce is perfect for dipping spring rolls, grilled chicken, or raw vegetables.
5. Store any leftovers in an airtight container in the refrigerator for up to 1 week.

NUTRITION INFORMATION PER SERVING
Calories: 100 | Protein: 4g | Fat: 7g | Carbs: 7g

BALSAMIC GLAZE

INGREDIENTS
- 1/2 cup balsamic vinegar
- 2 tbsp honey
- Salt to taste

Prep Time: 5 Min
Cook Time: 10 Min

Servings: 4

DIRECTIONS
1. Pour the balsamic vinegar and honey into a small saucepan and stir to combine.
2. Heat over medium-high heat, bringing it to a simmer.
3. Continue simmering for 8-10 minutes, stirring occasionally, until the mixture thickens to a syrupy consistency.
4. Remove from heat and allow the glaze to cool. It will continue to thicken as it cools.
5. Drizzle the balsamic glaze over salads, grilled vegetables, or roasted meats for a sweet and tangy flavor boost.

NUTRITION INFORMATION PER SERVING
Calories: 40 | Protein: 0g | Fat: 0g | Carbs: 11g

QUICK TOMATO SAUCE

INGREDIENTS
- 1 can (14 oz) crushed tomatoes
- 1 tbsp olive oil
- 1 clove garlic, minced
- 1 tsp dried basil
- 1/2 tsp dried oregano
- Salt and pepper to taste

Prep Time: 5 Min
Cook Time: 10 Min

Servings: 4

DIRECTIONS
1. Heat the olive oil in a saucepan over medium heat.
2. Add the minced garlic and sauté for 1 minute until fragrant.
3. Stir in the crushed tomatoes, basil, oregano, salt, and pepper.
4. Simmer for 8-10 minutes, stirring occasionally, until the sauce thickens slightly.
5. Taste and adjust the seasoning if needed. Serve over pasta, pizza, or as a dipping sauce for breadsticks.

NUTRITION INFORMATION PER SERVING
Calories: 60 | Protein: 2g | Fat: 3g | Carbs: 8g

AVOCADO LIME DRESSING

INGREDIENTS
- 1 ripe avocado
- 2 tbsp lime juice
- 2 tbsp olive oil
- 1 tbsp water
- Salt and pepper to taste

Prep Time: 5 Min
Cook Time: 0 Min

Servings: 4

DIRECTIONS
1. Scoop the avocado into a blender or food processor.
2. Add the lime juice, olive oil, and water, and blend until smooth.
3. Season with salt and pepper to taste.
4. If the dressing is too thick, add more water, one tablespoon at a time, until you reach your desired consistency.
5. Use this creamy dressing on salads, tacos, or grilled vegetables.

NUTRITION INFORMATION PER SERVING

Calories: 120 | Protein: 1g | Fat: 11g | Carbs: 8g

SPICY SRIRACHA MAYO

INGREDIENTS
- 1/2 cup mayonnaise
- 2 tbsp sriracha sauce
- 1 tsp lime juice
- 1/2 tsp garlic powder

Prep Time: 5 Min
Cook Time: 0 Min
Servings: 4

DIRECTIONS
1. In a small bowl, combine the mayonnaise, sriracha sauce, lime juice, and garlic powder.
2. Stir until the mixture is smooth and well combined.
3. Taste and adjust the level of spiciness by adding more sriracha if desired.
4. This spicy mayo is great for dipping fries, topping burgers, or drizzling on sushi rolls.

NUTRITION INFORMATION PER SERVING
Calories: 90 | Protein: 1g | Fat: 8g | Carbs: 3g

GARLIC PARMESAN SAUCE

INGREDIENTS
- 1/4 cup butter
- 2 cloves garlic, minced
- 1/4 cup grated Parmesan cheese
- 1 tbsp parsley, chopped
- Salt and pepper to taste

Prep Time: 5 Min
Cook Time: 5 Min

Servings: 4

DIRECTIONS
1. Melt the butter in a small saucepan over medium heat.
2. Add the minced garlic and sauté for 1-2 minutes until fragrant.
3. Stir in the Parmesan cheese and parsley, and season with salt and pepper.
4. Remove from heat and stir until the sauce is smooth.
5. This rich, savory sauce is perfect for pasta, grilled chicken, or drizzling over vegetables.

NUTRITION INFORMATION PER SERVING

Calories: 150 | Protein: 4g | Fat: 14g | Carbs: 2g

SIMPLE HONEY MUSTARD DRESSING

INGREDIENTS
- 2 tbsp Dijon mustard
- 2 tbsp honey
- 2 tbsp apple cider vinegar
- 1/4 cup olive oil
- Salt and pepper to taste

Prep Time: 5 Min
Cook Time: 0 Min

Servings: 4

DIRECTIONS
1. In a small bowl, whisk together the Dijon mustard, honey, and apple cider vinegar.
2. Slowly drizzle in the olive oil while continuing to whisk until the dressing is emulsified.
3. Season with salt and pepper to taste.
4. This tangy and sweet dressing is perfect for salads, as a dipping sauce for chicken, or drizzled over roasted vegetables.

NUTRITION INFORMATION PER SERVING
Calories: 80 | Protein: 1g | Fat: 7g | Carbs: 8g

TANGY TAHINI DRESSING

INGREDIENTS
- 1/4 cup tahini
- 2 tbsp lemon juice
- 2 tbsp olive oil
- 1 tbsp maple syrup
- 2 tbsp water
- Salt to taste

Prep Time: 5 Min
Cook Time: 0 Min

Servings: 4

DIRECTIONS
1. In a small bowl, combine tahini, lemon juice, olive oil, and maple syrup.
2. Add water a tablespoon at a time until you reach a smooth, pourable consistency.
3. Season with salt to taste.
4. This creamy tahini dressing is great for drizzling over salads, grain bowls, or roasted vegetables.

NUTRITION INFORMATION PER SERVING
Calories: 120 | Protein: 3g | Fat: 10g | Carbs: 6g

CLASSIC ITALIAN HERB SEASONING

INGREDIENTS
- 2 tbsp dried basil
- 2 tbsp dried oregano
- 1 tbsp dried thyme
- 1 tbsp garlic powder
- 1 tsp dried rosemary
- 1 tsp crushed red pepper flakes (optional)

Prep Time: 5 Min
Cook Time: 0 Min

Servings: 4

DIRECTIONS
1. In a small bowl, combine all the dried herbs and garlic powder.
2. Stir until the mixture is evenly blended.
3. Store in an airtight container for up to 6 months.
4. This versatile seasoning mix is perfect for seasoning pasta, pizza, roasted vegetables, or meats.

NUTRITION INFORMATION PER SERVING
Calories: 5 | Protein: 0g | Fat: 0g | Carbs: 1g

5-MINUTE PEANUT BUTTER DIPPING SAUCE

INGREDIENTS
- 1/4 cup peanut butter
- 2 tbsp soy sauce
- 1 tbsp honey
- 1 tsp rice vinegar
- 1/4 tsp garlic powder
- 2 tbsp warm water

Prep Time: 5 Min
Cook Time: 0 Min
Servings: 4

DIRECTIONS
1. In a small bowl, whisk together the peanut butter, soy sauce, honey, rice vinegar, and garlic powder.
2. Gradually add warm water, whisking until smooth and creamy.
3. Serve as a dipping sauce for vegetables, spring rolls, or grilled chicken.

NUTRITION INFORMATION PER SERVING
Calories: 120 | Protein: 4g | Fat: 9g | Carbs: 8g

SIMPLE LEMON GARLIC DRESSING

INGREDIENTS
- 3 tbsp fresh lemon juice
- 2 tbsp olive oil
- 1 clove garlic, minced
- 1 tsp Dijon mustard
- Salt and pepper to taste

Prep Time: 5 Min
Cook Time: 0 Min

Servings: 4

DIRECTIONS
1. In a small bowl, whisk together the lemon juice, olive oil, garlic, and Dijon mustard.
2. Season with salt and pepper to taste.
3. Drizzle over salads, roasted vegetables, or use as a marinade for fish or chicken.

NUTRITION INFORMATION PER SERVING

Calories: 60 | Protein: 1g | Fat: 5g | Carbs: 4g

SWEET CHILI SAUCE

INGREDIENTS

- 1/4 cup rice vinegar
- 2 tbsp soy sauce
- 2 tbsp honey
- 1 tbsp chili garlic sauce
- 1/2 tsp cornstarch (optional, for thicker sauce)

Prep Time: 5 Min
Cook Time: 5 Min

Servings: 4

DIRECTIONS

1. In a small saucepan, combine the rice vinegar, soy sauce, honey, and chili garlic sauce.
2. Bring to a simmer over medium heat.
3. If using cornstarch, mix it with a small amount of water and stir it into the sauce.
4. Simmer for 4-5 minutes, until the sauce thickens.
5. Allow to cool slightly before serving with spring rolls, grilled meats, or as a dipping sauce for crispy snacks.

NUTRITION INFORMATION PER SERVING
Calories: 45 | Protein: 1g | Fat: 0g | Carbs: 12g

METRIC SYSTEM

Temperatures

Celsius	Fan	Fahrenheit	Gas Mark
140C	Fan 120C	275F	Gas 1
150C	Fan 130C	300F	Gas 2
160C	Fan 140C	325F	Gas 3
170C	Fan 150C	340F	Gas 3
180C	Fan 160C	350F	Gas 4
190C	Fan 170C	375F	Gas 5
200C	Fan 180C	400F	Gas 6
220C	Fan 200C	425F	Gas 7
230C	Fan 210C	450F	Gas 8
240C	Fan 220C	475F	Gas 9

Measurements

Metric	Imperial
10 cm	4 in
12.5 cm	5 in
15 cm	6 in
18 cm	7 in
20 cm	8 in
23 cm	9 in
25 cm	10 in
30 cm	12 in

Spoons Sizes

Spoon Size	Milliliters
1 tsp	5 ml
2 tsp	10 ml
3 tsp	15 ml
3 tsp	1 tbsp
1 tbsp	15 ml

Baking Powder to Flour Ratio

Baking Powder	Flour
1 tsp	110 g
1 tsp	3.5 oz

Loaf Pan Sizes

Grams	Pounds
400 g	1 lb pan
900 g	1 kg/ 2 lb pan

NOTES

NOTES

NOTES

NOTES

NOTES

NOTES

NOTES

NOTES

NOTES

NOTES

Printed in Dunstable, United Kingdom